11:23

The Language of Faith

11:23

The Language of Faith

Mark Hankins

Mark Hankins Ministries

www.markhankins.org

CONTENTS

SECTION ONE
THE LAW OF FAITH:
ALL THINGS ARE POSSIBLE

If you only knew
what was on
the other
side of your
mountain

YOU
WOULD
MOVE
IT!

-Mark Hankins

(Mark 11:23)

Whosoever...
        shall have ...
                Whatsoever.

-Mark Hankins

Mark 11:23

For verily I say unto you, That whosoever shall say unto this mountain, Be thou removed, and be thou cast into the sea; and shall not doubt in his heart, but shall believe that those things which he saith shall come to pass; **he shall have whatsoever he saith.**

What Jesus did to the fig tree

in Mark 11:14

was not a

"Deity trick."

Mark 11:23 says,

"Whosoever shall say..."

-Mark Hankins

Mark 11:14

And Jesus answered and <u>said unto it</u>, No man eat fruit of thee hereafter for ever. And the disciples heard it.

If it was
God's will
for the mountain
to be there,
Jesus would not have
told you to move it.

-Mark Hankins

WORDS

are the building

blocks

of FAITH!

-Mark Hankins

When you begin

to say,

you are

<u>on the way</u>.

For verily I say [**<u>lego</u>** (Greek) - a systematic set discourse, building blocks] unto you, that whosoever shall say [**<u>epo</u>** (Greek) - command] unto this mountain, Be thou removed, and be thou cast into the sea; and shall not doubt in his heart, but shall believe that those things which he saith [**<u>laleo</u>** (Greek) - speak out] shall come to pass [a journey - on the way]; he shall have whatsoever he saith [**<u>lego</u>** (Greek) - a systematic set discourse, building blocks].

Mark 11:23 (Paraphrased)

Faith will not
necessarily

prevent

all mountains,

BUT IT WILL

MOVE THEM!

-Mark Hankins

Matthew 17:20

...verily I say unto you, If ye have faith as a grain
of mustard seed, ye shall say unto this mountain,
Remove hence to yonder place; and it shall remove;
and nothing shall be impossible unto you.

The reason
WORDS WILL MOVE
a mountain
is because
MOUNTAINS ARE
MADE
by
WORDS
-Mark Hankins

If you could find someone
WHOSE SPEECH
was perfectly true, you'd have
A PERFECT PERSON,
in perfect control of life.
A bit in the mouth of a horse
controls the whole horse.
A small rudder on a huge ship
in the hands of a skilled captain
sets course in the face of the
strongest wind.
A WORD
out of
YOUR MOUTH
may seem of no account,
but it can accomplish nearly
everything – or destroy it!

James 3:2-5 (The Message)

Words are powerful; take them seriously. Words can be your salvation. Words can also be your damnation.

Matthew 12:37
(The Message)

For by your words you will be justified and acquitted, and by your words you will condemned and sentenced.

Matthew 12:37

(Amplified)

There are
NO
IMMOVABLE
mountains.

-Mark Hankins

=====

Matthew 21:21

...Verily I say unto you, If ye have faith and doubt not, ye shall not only do this which is done to the fig tree, but also if ye shall say unto this mountain, Be thou removed, and be thou cast into the sea; it shall be done.

If the mountain is there, you can move it.

-Mark Hankins

Your mountain needs to hear your voice.
-Mark Hankins

• • • • • • • • • • • • • •

Jesus did not say he shall have whatsoever he **THINKETH**, but he shall have whatsoever he **SAITH**.

-Mark Hankins

If your faith isn't talking,

it isn't working.

Faith always has

a voice.

-Mark Hankins

● ● ● ● ● ● ● ● ● ● ● ● ● ● ● ●

Luke 17:5,6

And the apostles said unto the Lord, Increase our faith. And the Lord said, If ye had faith as a grain of mustard seed, ye might say unto this sycamine tree, Be thou plucked up by the root, and be thou planted in the sea; and it should obey you.

CHANGE

your

WORDS

and

CHANGE

your

WORLD.

-Mark Hankins

Hebrews 11:3

Through faith we understand that the worlds were framed by the word of God, so that things which are seen were not made of things which do appear.

If what you
have
in life is all up
to God,
Jesus never
would have said
Mark 11:23.

-**Mark Hankins**

SECTION TWO
THE SPIRIT OF FAITH:

BELIEVE AND SPEAK

The spirit of faith will make you swing out over hell on a cornstalk and spit in the devil's eye!

-Mark Hankins

Luke 10:19

Behold, I give unto you power to tread on serpents and scorpions, and over all the power of the enemy: and nothing shall by any means hurt you.

The
spirit of faith
will make a
tadpole
slap a
whale!
-Mark Hankins

2 Corinthians 4:13

We having the same spirit of faith, according as it is written, I believed, and therefore have I spoken; we also believe, and therefore speak.

The principles of faith are taught.

The spirit of faith is caught.

The spirit of faith is contagious.

The spirit of faith is more than just a formula; it is a fire in the spirit of man.

-Mark Hankins

The spirit of faith affects every area of your life.

-Mark Hankins

Faith will work for anyone and will work on **anything.**

-Mark Hankins

The door to the
supernatural has
one knob,
and it is on
your side
of the door.

-Mark Hankins

The door to the
supernatural swings
on two hinges...
Believing and Speaking.

-Kenneth E. Hagin

Your faith

will never rise above

your words.

-Mark Hankins

If you're not happy with what you have in life, check out what you've been saying.

-Mark Hankins

Mark 11:24

...What things soever ye desire, when ye pray, believe that ye receive them, and ye shall have them.

The spirit of faith will
ANNOUNCE

the

OUTCOME

in the middle of

ADVERSITY.

-Mark Hankins

Acts 27:25

...for I believe God, that it shall
be even as it was told me.

It's not necessary, unless it's necessary.
– B. B. Hankins

Faith will cause you to shout

while the walls are still standing;

it will cause you to dance like

David did when the ark of the

covenant was returned to Jerusalem

and the glory returned; it may cause

you to run like Elijah did when the

hand of the Lord

came upon him; it may cause you to

sing and praise God loudly as Paul

and Silas did at midnight when they

were imprisoned in chains.

-Mark Hankins

SECTION THREE
THE BELIEVER'S VOICE

Your words can **limit you** or **loose you!**

-Mark Hankins

Proverbs 6:2

Thou art snared by the words of thy mouth, thou art taken with the words of thy mouth.

Your voice is **your address** in the realm of the spirit.

-Mark Hankins

Acts 16:25-26

And at midnight, Paul and Silas prayed, and sang praises unto God...and suddenly there was a great earthquake and every [prisoner's] bands were loosed.

Satan should have taped their mouths shut...As long as you can move your mouth, you can move a mountain.

Praising God is an act of faith and will release your faith.

-Mark Hankins

Get a grip on your lip!

CONFESSION

always

precedes and sustains

possession.

-Mark Hankins

Hebrews 10:23

Let us hold fast the profession of our faith without wavering; (for he is faithful that promised).

Confession builds the road over which faith carries its mighty cargo.

- E.W. Kenyon

Hebrews 3:1

Wherefore, holy brethren, partakers of the heavenly calling, consider the Apostle and High Priest of our profession, Christ Jesus.

The speech center is the dominion center for our lives.

-Mark Hankins

(James 3:2-5)

Proverbs 18:21

Death and life are in the power of the tongue: and they that love it shall eat the fruit thereof.

If you are
silent,
you lose
by default.
**Faith works by
speaking.**

-Mark Hankins

Never run
at your
GIANT
with your
MOUTH
shut!!!

-Mark Hankins

Winning the war of words is necessary to win the fight of faith.

-Mark Hankins

I Samuel 17:37

David said moreover, The Lord that delivered me out of the paw of the lion, and out of the paw of the bear, he will deliver me out of the hand of this Philistine.

JESUS WON the war of words.

-Mark Hankins

It is written...

It is written...

It is said...

[the devil] departed from [Jesus] for a season.

(Luke 4:4-13)

Nothing will
establish
you
and
build your faith
as quickly as
confession.

-F.F. Bosworth

The reason the majority of
Christians are weak,

though they are

sincere, is because

they have

never dared

to make a

bold confession

of who they are

in Christ.

- E.W. Kenyon

Our identification

with Christ

demands

the identical

confession of faith.

-Mark Hankins

Philemon 6

That the communication of thy faith may become effectual by the acknowledging of every good thing which is in you in Christ Jesus.

I am who God says I am.

I have what God says I have.

I can do what God says I can do.

SECTION FOUR
FAITH AND ACTION

FAITH

is an act:

The simplest definition of faith is acting

like the Bible is true.

-Mark Hankins

Hebrews 11:4, 5, 8, 20, 21, 22, 23, 29, 31

(The Message)

"By an act of faith...."

Faith

without

corresponding

action

is dead.

-Mark Hankins

James 2:18

(Weymouth)

...prove to me your faith apart from corresponding actions and I will prove mine to you by my actions.

FAITH has a VOCAL and BODY language.

-Mark Hankins

The spirit of faith can be seen and heard.

-Mark Hankins

Luke 5:20

And when He saw their faith, He said....

Your
faith
must move
your
mouth
before it moves
your
mountain.

-Mark Hankins

Faith moves God.

Faith moves mountains.

Faith won't move anything

until it moves <u>you</u>.

The first part of you that
your faith will move is

<u>your mouth</u>.

God is a faith God.

-Mark Hankins

Hebrews 11:6

But without faith it is impossible to
please Him....

You will have to carry
dead faith,
but
living faith
will carry you.

-Mark Hankins

When you see the
invisible, you can do the
impossible.

-Oral Roberts

James 2:17

Even so faith, if it hath not works, is dead....

Dead faith
is about as
good
to you as a
dead Jesus.
-Mark Hankins

Jesus is alive
and so should your
faith be.

-Mark Hankins

The

Holy Spirit

will always

prompt

you to

act in faith,

but your act is

opening the door for

God's act.

-Mark Hankins

The Holy Spirit

is a **GENIUS**;

if you'll listen to Him

He will make you

look smart.

-B.B. Hankins

The Holy Spirit lands where the Word of God is spoken.

-Mark Hankins

While Peter was still speaking these words, the Holy Spirit fell upon all those who heard the word.

Acts 10:44

Don't doubt, just shout, and God will work it all out!

-David Shearin

May God help us to understand this....
It is time people knew how to
<u>SHOUT IN FAITH</u>
as they contemplate the
ETERNAL POWER
of our God...
I come across some who
would be giants in the
power of God,
but they
have no
<u>SHOUT OF FAITH</u>.

-Smith Wigglesworth

For those tough stains you
have to **"Shout"** them out!

-Mark Hankins

FAITH AIN'T PRETTY!

- Mark Hankins

I Corinthians 1:27

But God hath chosen the foolish things of the world to confound the wise; and God hath chosen the weak things of the world to confound the things which are mighty.

Some people would

have great faith,

but they are too

self-conscious to

"GET UGLY" for

Jesus.

-Mark Hankins

Acts of God
are precipitated by
acts of faith.

Your act is the opening act for
the main event:

God's act!

-Mark Hankins

Acts 10:19,20

...the Spirit said...

Arise

...go with them, doubting
nothing....

Some people are **self-conscious.**

Some people are **people-conscious.**

Some people are **devil-conscious**.

Some people are **un-conscious.**

Faith is God-Conscious!

-Mark Hankins

SECTION FIVE
CORPORATE FAITH

FAITH
is a
TEAM SPORT.

-Mark Hankins

(Hebrews 10:25)

Everyone needs at least four **"crazy" friends** who believe that **with God** all things are possible.

-Mark Hankins

Mark 2:3 (NKJV)

Then they came to Him, bringing a paralytic who was carried by four men.

You need to form a faith gang.

-Mark Hankins

Some **ASSEMBLY** required.

-Mark Hankins

Acts 4:31

And when they had prayed, the place was shaken where they were **ASSEMBLED** together; and they were all filled with the Holy Ghost, and they spake the word of God with boldness.

If the devil can
trick
you into being
independent,
he can get you out
of a place of faith.

-Smith Wigglesworth

SECTION SIX
THE WORD OF FAITH

When faith cometh...

FEAR

GOETH!

-Mark Hankins

---

2 Timothy 1:7

For God hath not given us the spirit of fear; but of power, and of love, and of a sound mind.

When faith cometh...

You

knoweth!

-Mark Hankins

Romans 10:17

So then faith cometh by hearing, and hearing by the Word of God.

====

Jesus said to me,

"My words

in your mouth

are just as

powerful

as My words in

My mouth."

-Reinhard Bonnke

The Word of God spoken to you must be spoken through you.

-Mark Hankins

Acts 27:25

...for I believe God, that it shall be even as it was told me.

The

Word of God

was spoken before

it was written,

and it was written

so it

could be spoken.

-Mark Hankins

Matthew 4:4

...It is written, Man shall not live by bread alone, but by every word that proceedeth out of the mouth of God.

The whole Bible

is not about faith, but the

whole Bible

does have the capacity to

produce faith

for whatever you need to

receive from God.

-Mark Hankins

2 Peter 1:3-4

...as His divine power hath given unto us all things that pertain unto life and godliness, through the knowledge of him that hath called us to glory and virtue...are given unto us exceeding great and precious promises....

It is impossible to **boldly claim** by faith a blessing that you are not sure God is offering.

-F.F. Bosworth

I John 5:14,15

And this is the confidence that we have in him, that, if we ask any thing according to His will, He heareth us: And if we know that He hear us, whatsoever we ask, we know that we have the petitions that we desired of him.

God delights in His children stepping out over the aching void with nothing under their feet but the **Word of God.**

- Dr. Lilian B. Yeomans

====

When you put

God's Word

in your mouth, you're

breathing in the

life of God.

-Mark Hankins

2 Timothy 3:16 (NIV)

All Scripture is God-breathed and is
useful for teaching, rebuking, correcting,
and training in righteousness.

God's Word

in your mouth

is

mouth-to-mouth

resuscitation

from God.

-Mark Hankins

SECTION SEVEN

HOLY SPIRIT...

SPEECH THERAPY

Our only safeguard from dropping back into our natural mind with which we can receive nothing from God is by being filled and filled again with the Holy Spirit.

-Smith Wigglesworth

Ephesians 5:18-19

And be not drunk with wine, wherein is excess; but be filled with the Spirit; Speaking to yourselves in psalms and hymns and spiritual songs, singing and making melody in your heart to the Lord.

The Holy Ghost will

always

move you to

speak!

-Mark Hankins

---

2 Peter 1:21

For the prophecy came not in old time by the will of man: but holy men of God spake as they were moved by the Holy Ghost.

God's head-bypass operation:

Speaking in the Holy Ghost.

-Mark Hankins

For if I pray in a unknown tongue, my spirit prayeth, but my understanding is unfruitful.

1 Corinthians 14:14

Holy Spirit Speech Therapy:

Speaking...is a means of

spiritual edification

and

supernatural communication

with God.

-Mark Hankins

I Corinthians 14:2-4

For he that speaketh in an unknown tongue speaketh not unto men, but unto God...in the spirit he speaketh mysteries...He that speaketh in an unknown tongue edifieth himself....

SECTION EIGHT
THE GOD-KIND OF FAITH

The God-kind of faith
is not an
accessory or an
option; it is an
absolute

necessity!
-Mark Hankins

God demands faith of us. He has given
us the means whereby we can get faith.
-Mark Hankins

So then faith comes by hearing, and
hearing by the word of God.

Romans 10:17

Hebrews 11:6

But without faith it is impossible to please him:
for he that cometh to God must believe that
He is, and that He is a rewarder of them that
diligently seek Him.

EVERY
born-again believer
has a measure of
mountain moving
faith.

-Mark Hankins

Romans 12:3

For I say, through the grace given unto me, to every man that is among you, not to think of himself more highly than he ought to think; but to think soberly, according as God hath dealt to every man the measure of faith.

With God it is not just

what you can

believe for,

but what you can

obey for.

-Mark Hankins

Hebrews 11:8a

By faith Abraham, when he was called to go out into a place which he should after receive for an inheritance, obeyed....

Faith is obeying God even when there is an element of the unknown.

-Mark Hankins

Hebrews 11:8

By faith Abraham...went out, not knowing whither he went.

Sometimes a stretch of water must be walked on before you can get to Jesus for the miracle you need.

-Lilian B. Yeomans

Matthew 14:29b

...And when Peter was come down out of the ship, he walked on the water, to go to Jesus.

Any time

GOD WANTS

to change someone's

LIFE,

He always touches

THEIR MOUTH.

-Mark Hankins

Jeremiah 1:9

Then the Lord put forth his hand, and touched my mouth. And the Lord said unto me, Behold, I have put my words in thy mouth.

Living by faith

is not something

you

do every once in a

while; it's a daily

walk with God.

-Mark Hankins

Romans 1:17

...The just shall live by faith.

God's plan
for your life
requires
you to
WALK BY
FAITH!

-Mark Hankins

(2 Corinthians 5:7)

Section Nine
Faith...Love...Joy

The

biggest

enemy to faith

is

UNFORGIVENESS.

-Mark Hankins

Mark 11:25

And when ye stand praying, forgive, if ye have ought against any: that your Father also which is in heaven may forgive you your trespasses.

You may be

able to

WHIP A SKUNK,

but you might not

want to!

-Mark Hankins

I Peter 2:23 (Phillips)

Yet when he was insulted he offered no insult in return. When he suffered he made no threats of revenge. He simply committed his cause to the one who judges fairly.

Faith works by love.

A step out of love is a step out of God.

-Kenneth E. Hagin

Galatians 5:6

(Amplified)

...faith [is] activated and energized and expressed and working through love.

Satan is impatient.

You can

OUTLAST

him.

-Jesse Duplantis

Hebrews 6:12

...through faith and patience inherit the promises.

Your enemy, the devil, does not have any of the fruit of the spirit.

Develop the fruit of the spirit and you will overcome.

-Mark Hankins

Galatians 5:22, 23

But the fruit of the Spirit is love, joy, peace, long suffering, gentleness, goodness, faith, meekness, temperance....

Any man may be CHANGED BY FAITH no matter how he may be fettered.

- Smith Wigglesworth

I John 5:4

For whatsoever is born of God overcometh the world: and this is the victory that overcometh the world, even our faith.

Whenever you believe God, you always CHEER UP!

-Mark Hankins

Acts 27:25

Wherefore, sirs, be of good cheer: for I believe God, that it shall be even as it was told me.

FAITH...LOVE...JOY

JOY

is the

BRIDGE

between

believing and

receiving.

-Mark Hankins

I Peter 1:8-9

... yet believing, ye rejoice with joy unspeakable and full of glory: receiving the end of your faith....

SECTION TEN

FAITH:

THE DOOR TO THE SUPERNATURAL

Just because you know how

faith works

doesn't mean you

know how

God is going to do your **miracle.**

-Mark Hankins

(Romans 11:33)

Luke 1:45

And blessed is she that believed: for there shall be a performance of those things which were told her from the Lord.

There is no pressure on you to MAKE IT HAPPEN. The only pressure on you is to believe.

- Patsy Cameneti

Hebrews 4:3

For we which have believed do enter into rest....

Keep the

FAITH SWITCH

turned on!

-Mark Hankins

You are the

BELIEVER

and

God is the performer.

-Mark Hankins

====

Romans 4:20-21

He staggered not at the promise of God through unbelief; but was strong in faith, giving glory to God; And being fully persuaded that, what He had promised, He was able also to perform.

The SAME FAITH that makes you whole... keeps you WHOLE.

-Mark Hankins

Mark 5:34

And He said unto her, "Daughter, thy faith hath made thee whole; go in peace, and be whole of thy plague."

If you don't see any

GLORY,

you'd better

check your "believer"
because if you do believe,

YOU WILL SEE

the glory.

-Mark Hankins

John 11:40

Jesus saith unto her, "Said I not unto
thee, that, if thou wouldest believe, thou
shouldest see the glory of God?"

Make sure your "speaker" is HOOKED UP to your "believer."

-Mark Hankins

2 Corinthians 4:13 [NEB]

But Scripture says, "I believed, and therefore I spoke out," and we, too, in the same spirit of faith, believe and therefore speak out....

God has tied Himself irrevocably

to human cooperation

in the execution of

divine purposes.

He has made man's faith

a determining factor

in the work of redemption.

-Dr. Lilian B. Yeomans

A man gets what he believes for in life -
nothing more, nothing less.

- Kenneth E. Hagin

Matthew 9:29

...According to your faith be it unto you.

There are four kinds of expectation:

One: Positive

Two: Negative

Three: Misguided

Four: Neutral

- Mac Hammond

Psalm 62:5

My soul, wait thou only upon God; for my expectation is from Him.

SECTION ELEVEN
PIONEER FAITH

The spirit of faith will make you leave your COMFORT ZONE.

-Mark Hankins

Hebrews 11:24-25

By faith Moses, when he was come to years, refused to be called the son of Pharaoh's daughter; Choosing rather to suffer affliction with the people of God, than to enjoy the pleasures of sin for a season.

The
SPIRIT OF FAITH
is a
PIONEER SPIRIT.

-Mark Hankins

Hebrews 11:8

By faith Abraham...went out, not knowing whither he went.

There are three kinds of people:

Pioneers,
Settlers, &
Museum Keepers.

Museum keepers are content to dust off the memories of the past.

Settlers are content to stay in their comfort zone.

Pioneers are constantly pressing into new territories.

-Mark Hankins

SECTION TWELVE
WINNING THE FAITH FIGHT

The faith fight is the only fight believers are called to fight.

-Mark Hankins

I Timothy 6:12

Fight the good fight of faith, lay hold on eternal life, where unto thou art also called, and hast professed a good profession before many witnesses.

It takes faith

to go where God wants

you to go, and

it takes faith

to stay where God wants

you to stay.

-Mark Hankins

Genesis 26:2,3

And the Lord appeared unto [Isaac], and said, "Go not down into Egypt; dwell in the land which I shall tell thee of: Sojourn in this land, and I will be with thee, and will bless thee...."

If you will keep your faith, your faith will keep you.

-Mark Hankins

2 Timothy 4:7

I have fought a good fight, I have finished my course, I have kept the faith.

"The Word that saves us is right here, as near as the tongue in your mouth, as close as the heart in your chest." It's the word of faith that welcomes God to go to work and set things right for us. This is the core of our preaching. Say the welcoming word to God- "Jesus is my Master"-embracing, body and soul, God's work of doing in us what he did in raising Jesus from the dead. That's it. You're not "doing" anything; you're simply calling out to God, trusting him to do it for you. That's salvation. With your whole being you embrace God setting things right, and then you say it, right out loud: "God has set everything right between him and me!"

Romans 10:8-10

(The Message)

That if thou shalt confess with thy mouth the Lord Jesus, and shalt believe in thine heart that God raised Him from the dead, thou shalt be saved.

Romans 10:9

NEVER
Underestimate
the
POWER
of
ONE VOICE

-Mark Hankins

...The voice of
one crying in the
wilderness, Prepare
ye the way of the Lord...

Luke 3:4

...lift up thy voice with
strength; lift it up, be
not afraid; say unto the
cities...behold your God.

Isaiah 40:3-9

SECTION THIRTEEN
FAITH IN THE BLOOD

WHOM GOD SET FORTH TO BE A
PROPITIATION, THROUGH FAITH IN HIS
BLOOD, TO DECLARE HIS
RIGHTEOUSNESS,
FOR THE REMISSION OF SINS THAT
ARE PAST, THROUGH THE
FORBEARANCE OF GOD.

-ROMANS 3:25

The BLOOD OF JESUS is **liquid love** that flows from the heart of God and reaches into the heart of man and **heals** us where we have been wounded by life.

-Mark Hankins

Where the blood of Jesus is honored, the Holy Spirit will work. The Holy Spirit goes where the blood flows.
-Mark Hankins

There's not one thing in me that the blood does not cleanse.
-Smith Wigglesworth

Faith in the Blood-
PLUS NOTHING,
MINUS NOTHING-
is all you need to enjoy
God's best blessings.
-Mark Hankins

For the enjoyment of this
blessedness,
nothing is neccessary except
faith in the blood.
The blood alone has done
everything.
-Andrew Murray

Neither by the blood of goats and calves, but by His own blood He entered in once into the holy place, having obtained eternal redemption for us.

Hebrews 9:12

God is on my side,
for the blood has been applied.
Every need shall be supplied
and nothing shall be denied.
So I enter into rest,
and I know that I am blessed.
I have passed the test
and I will get God's best.

-Trina Hankins

Mark and Trina Hankins travel nationally and internationally preaching the Word of God with the power of the Holy Spirit. Their message centers on the spirit of faith, the identify of the believer in Christ, and the work of the Holy Spirit.

After over 35 years of pastoral and traveling ministry, Mark and Trina are now ministering full-time in campmeetings, leadership conferences, and church services around the world and across the United States. Their son Aaron Hankins and his wife Errin Cody are now the pastors of Christian Worship Center in Alexandria, Louisiana. Their daughter Alica Moran and her husband Caleb pastor Metro Life Church in Lafayette, Louisiana. Mark and Trina also have five grandchildren.

Mark is also the author of several books. For more information on Mark Hankins Ministries please log on to our website, **www.markhankins.org.**

Acknowledgements
Special Thanks To:
My wife, Trina
My son, Aaron, and his wife Errin Cody
Their children Avery Jane,
Macy Claire, and Jude Aaron
My daughter, Alicia, and her husband Caleb
Their children Jaiden Mark and Gavin Luke
My parents, Pastors B.B. and Velma Hankins,
who are now in Heaven with the Lord
My wife's parents, Rev. William and Ginger Behrman.

Purchasing and Contact Information

Mark Hankins Ministries

PO Box 12863

Alexandria, LA 71315

Phone: 318.448.4500

Fax: 318.443.2948

E-mail:contact@markhankins.org

Visit us on the web:
www.markhankins.org

Books by Mark Hankins

Spirit-Filled Scripture Study Guide - $35
This is a comprehensive study of scriptures in over 120 different translations covering many topics including: redemption, faith, finances, and prayer.

The Spirit of Faith - $15
If you only knew what was on the other side of your mountain you would move it! Having a spirit of faith is necessary to do the will of God and fulfill your destiny. The Spirit of faith turns defeat into victory and dreams into reality.

The Bloodline of a Champion - $15
The blood of Jesus is "liquid love" that flows from the heart of God and gives us hope in all circumstances. In this book we will be studying the power of the blood of Jesus. Not only will we clearly see what the blood has done for us, but also what it does in us as believers.

Taking Your Place In Christ - $12.50
Many Christians talk about what they are trying to be and what they are going to be. This book is about who you are now as a believer in Christ.

Paul's System of Truth - $15
Paul's System of Truth reveals man's condition in Christ, the reality of what happened from the cross to the throne and how it is applied for victory in our life through Jesus Christ. This book will revolutionize your view of who you are and what you have in Christ.

For more information:
www.markhankins.org

Let the Good Times Roll - $12.50

This book focuses on the five keys to Heaven on earth: The Holy Spirit, glory, faith, joy, and redemption. The Holy Spirit is a genius. if you will listen to Him, He will make you look smart.

Revolutionary Revelation - $12.50

This book provides excellent insight on how the spirit of wisdom and revelation is mandatory for believers to access their call, inheritance, and authority in Christ.

The Power of Identification With Christ - $15

This book focuses on the reality of redemption and your new identity in Christ. As a new creature, you have everything you need inside of you to succeed in life!

Never Run at Your Giant With Your Mouth Shut - $5

When David ran at Goliath, there was a war of words going on. In this book, we learn that winning the war of words is necessary to winning the fight of faith.

Acknowledging Every Good Thing That Is In You In Christ - $2.50

This mini-book encourages every believer to have a daily confession or acknowledgment of who they are in Christ.

FOR MORE INFORMATION:
WWW.MARKHANKINS.ORG